MENDELSSOHN

ALLEGRO BRILLANT
OPUS 92
FOR ONE PIANO, FOUR HANDS

MW01130150

EDITED BY MAURICE HINSON AND ALLISON NELSON

AN ALFRED MASTERWORK EDITION

Alfred Music Publishing Co., Inc.
P.O. Box 10003
Van Nuys, CA 91410-0003
alfred.com

Cover art: Bay of Amalfi
by Felix Mendelssohn
watercolor, c.1830
Bodleian Library
University of Oxford, Oxford

Copyright © MMXI by Alfred Music Publishing Co., Inc.
All rights reserved. Printed in USA.

ISBN-10: 0-7390-7912-3
ISBN-13: 978-0-7390-7912-6

FELIX MENDELSSOHN

ALLEGRO BRILLANT, OP. 92 (FOR ONE PIANO, FOUR HANDS)

Edited by Maurice Hinson and Allison Nelson

Foreword

ABOUT THE COMPOSER AND THIS EDITION

Felix Mendelssohn (1809–1847) had a long relationship with piano duets. From his very early teens, he wrote original works for piano four hands and played duets with his sister Fanny (1805–1847), also a talented pianist and composer. His output of four-hand works includes arrangements of his symphonies, overtures, chamber music, and seven of the *Songs without Words*. In 1833, he collaborated with his friend, the Bohemian pianist, composer, and teacher Ignaz Moscheles (1794–1870), on the *Variations on a Theme by Weber*, Op. 87b, for two pianos, four hands.

His two most impressive works for four hands are the *Andante and Variations*, Op. 83a, and the *Andante and Allegro brillant*, Op. 92 (generally known as the *Allegro brillant*). The Op. 83a has its inspiration in a solo work of the same name, sharing the theme and a couple of variations. It seems that the Op. 92 is Mendelssohn's only significant duet composition that does not have a connection to another version.

The Op. 92 has an interesting history that begins with an autograph dated March 23, 1841, located in the Biblioteka Jagiellonska in Cracow, Poland. The work is in Mendelssohn's handwriting and is titled *Allegro assai vivace*.

A second autograph of the same work, dated by Mendelssohn March 26, 1841, and located in the Biblioteque Nationale in Paris, is written in oblong format with the Secondo part to the left and the Primo to the right. This autograph opens with an introductory *Andante* leading into the *Allegro assai vivace*.

The third source, located in the Staatsbibliotek in Berlin, is a copy of the Paris autograph but is written in another person's hand.

This current edition is based on the second source, the Paris autograph. Mendelssohn dedicated the Op. 92 to Clara Schumann (1819–1896). He composed it "expressly to play with his friend" at her concert on March 31, 1841. *Allegro brillant* is one of the most challenging pieces in the entire piano duet repertoire.

ABOUT THE MUSIC

Form: Introduction = measures 1–53 (through-composed).

The expressive opening *Andante* is one of Mendelssohn's most effective slow and introspective introductions. It is essential to the virtuosic *Allegro assai vivace*, making the work much more complete and effective.

Form: **A** = measures 54–132; **B** = 133–upbeat to 172; A^1 = 173–229; A^2 = 230–downbeat of 279; B^1 = upbeat to 280–downbeat of 381; B^2 = upbeat to 382–417; coda = upbeat to 418–482.

The *Allegro assai vivace* at first appears to be a sonata-allegro design but closer inspection reveals two large sections (**A, B**) that have been reworked and repeated, leading to a brilliant and impetuous coda. This virtuosic work is full of fast scales and arpeggiated passages, and also includes some antiphonal sections.

EDITORIAL AND PERFORMANCE CONSIDERATIONS

This duet is a performing edition. There were several omissions in the Paris manuscript that include accidentals, slurs, clefs, and other notation, most of which have been supplemented by the editors. All fingering and metronome markings are also editorial suggestons, which can be adjusted to suit the performers' technique. In several passages, the Primo part is written in octaves or chords at the low end of the keyboard. The editors have included suggestions for redistribution to help make those physically uncomfortable passages more accessible.

Pedaling is very challenging. In the *Andante*, the melody alternates between the Primo and Secondo parts—one part rests while the other plays; therefore, the players must also alternate using the pedal. While not very practical, to manage the legato most effectively, the Primo (who is primarily pedaling) must learn how to pedal for the Secondo solos. This same situation arises in the lyrical section of the *Allegro assai vivace*.

SOURCES CONSULTED

Lubin, Ernest. *The Piano Duet.* New York: Grossman Publishers, 1970.

McGraw, Cameron. *Piano Duet Repertoire.* Bloomington: Indiana University Press, 1981.

Mendelssohn, Felix. *Werke für Klavier zu vier Händen.* München: Henle Verlag, 1994.

Sadie, Stanley (editor). *The New Grove Dictionary of Music and Musicians.* London: Macmillan Publishers Limited, 1980.

Todd, R. Larry. *Mendelssohn: A Life in Music.* New York: Oxford University Press, 2003.

Andante und Allegro assai vivace

SECONDO

Felix Mendelssohn (1809–1847)
Op. 92

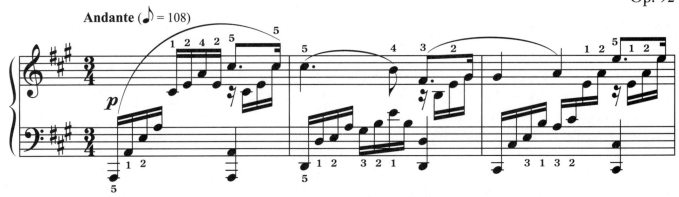

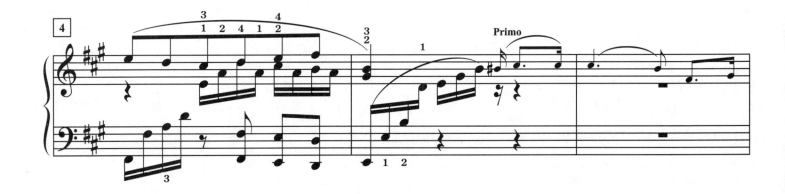

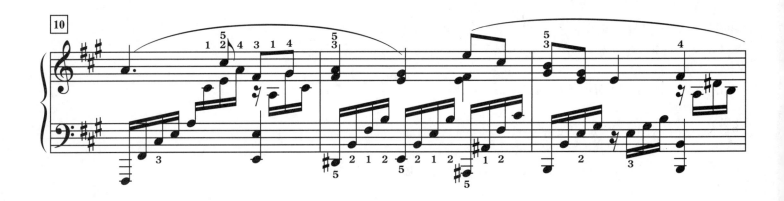

Andante und Allegro assai vivace

PRIMO

Felix Mendelssohn (1809–1847)
Op. 92

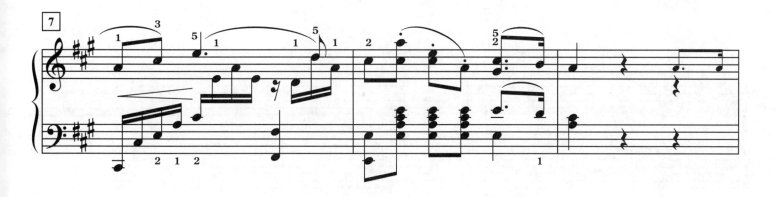

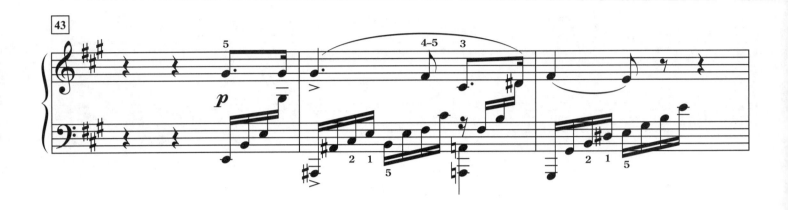

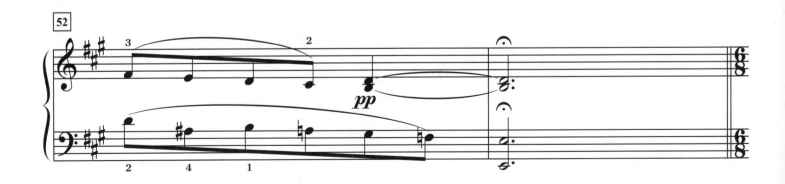

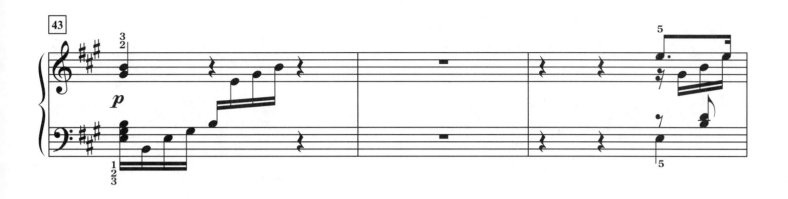

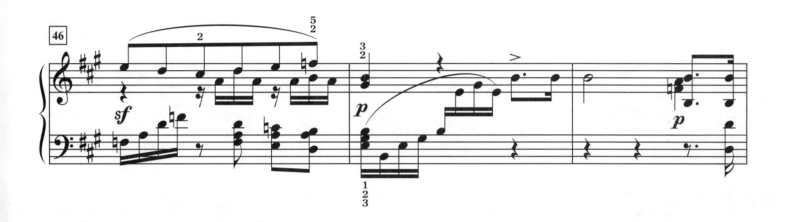

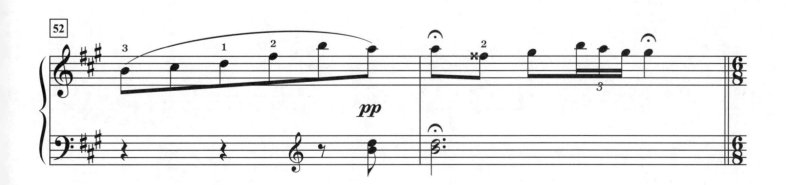

* In the manuscript, the staccato marks become irregular from this point on.
  Keep the same performance pattern throughout.

* In the manuscript, the staccato marks become irregular from this point on.
  Keep the same performance pattern throughout.

* From here to m. 169, the RH is at an awkward angle to the keyboard. For a more comfortable performance,
  the upper staff notes can be divided between the hands while the lower staff can be played by the Secondo.

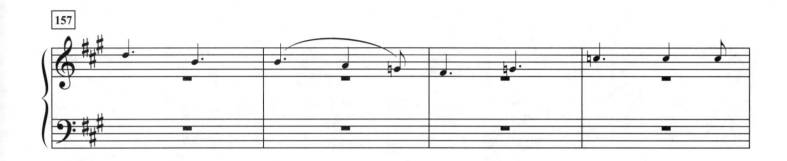

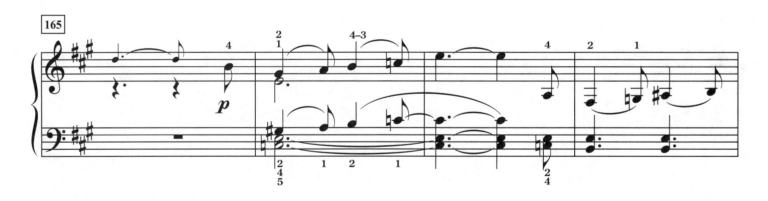

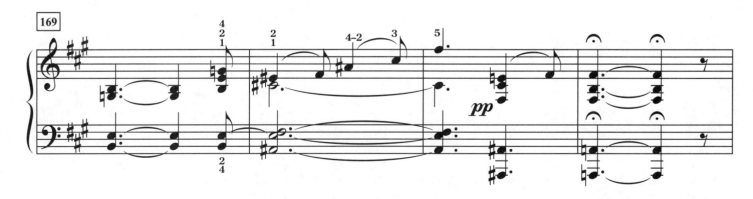

* Primo LH crosses Secondo RH.

* Primo LH crosses Secondo's RH.

* Primo LH doubles melody in Secondo.

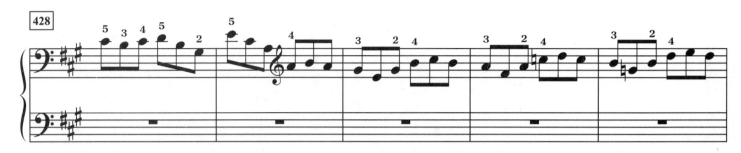